SECOND EDITION

Workbook

2

SUPER MINDS

Herbert Puchta · Peter Lewis-Jones · Günter Gerngross · Helen Kidd

CAMBRIDGE
UNIVERSITY PRESS

Contents

Back to School

1 **Look and match.**

wall   board   bookcase   cabinet   door

clock   window   crayon   chair   floor

1 Look, read, and check ☑.

1 There's an apple.   yes ☑   no ☐

2 There's a clock.   yes ☐   no ☐

3 There's a lizard.   yes ☐   no ☐

4 There are some books.   yes ☐   no ☐

5 There are some rulers.   yes ☐   no ☐

6 There's a board.   yes ☐   no ☐

2 Read and circle.

(1) **There's** / **There are** a hat on the floor.

(2) **There's** / **There are** some pictures on the wall.

(3) **There's** / **There are** a bed by the door.

3 Write about your classroom.

1 There _____ a _____.

2 There _____ some _____.

1 🎧 001 Can you remember? Listen and write.

eighty-eight   sixty-six   thirty-three   ~~twenty-two~~

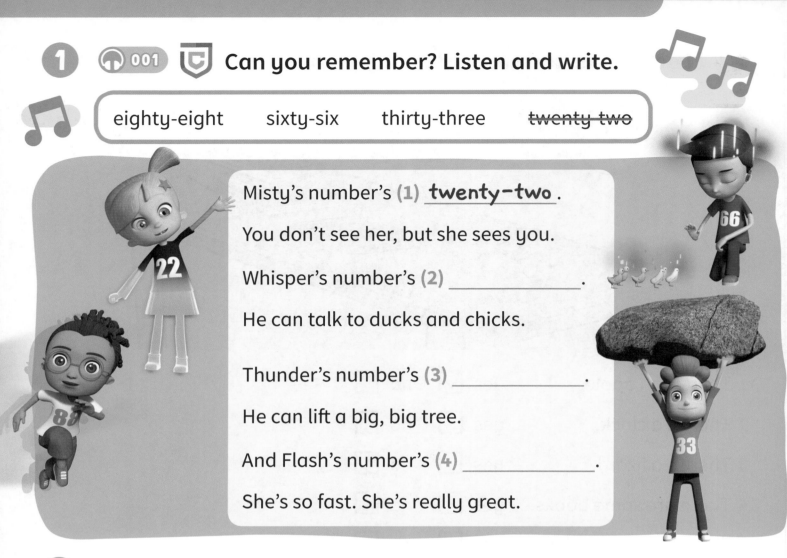

Misty's number's (1) __twenty-two__.

You don't see her, but she sees you.

Whisper's number's (2) _____.

He can talk to ducks and chicks.

Thunder's number's (3) _____.

He can lift a big, big tree.

And Flash's number's (4) _____.

She's so fast. She's really great.

2 Look and match.

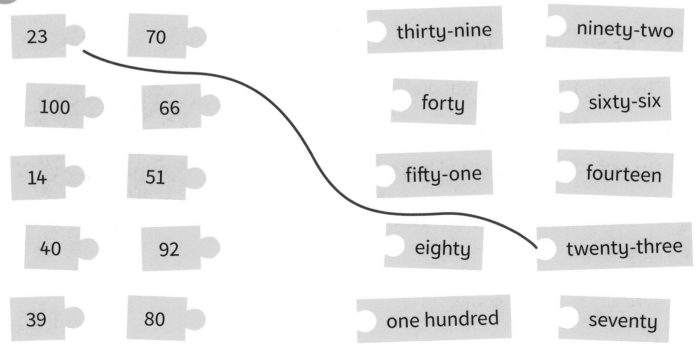

23	70	thirty-nine	ninety-two
100	66	forty	sixty-six
14	51	fifty-one	fourteen
40	92	eighty	twenty-three
39	80	one hundred	seventy

Write the words in the correct order.

1 up / Please / stand

> _Please stand up_ .

2 sit / Don't / down

> _____ .

3 book / your / Open

> _____ .

4 stand / Don't / up

> _____ .

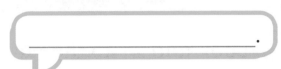 **Look at Activity 1. Number the pictures.**

☐ ☐ ☐ [1]

Look and write.

don't   ~~open~~   sit down   stand up

(1) **Open** _____ the book.

Open the book, please.

(2) Stand up. _____ , please.

(3) _____ sit down!

(4) Don't _____ , please!

Yes!

1 🎧 002 **Who says it? Listen and check ☑.**

1

2

3

2 🛡 **Look and write the numbers.**

1 — I have an idea. Wait here!

3 — Can you check this out, Flash?

2 — Great work.

4 — We have them!

a ____

b __1__

c ____

d ____

1 **Write and circle.**

1 I can write the names of five things in a classroom.   **Yes** / **No**

door _____ _____ _____ _____ _____

2 Which number comes …

after eleven? _____

after ninety-nine? _____

3 There **is** / **are** some pencils.

2 **Look and write the numbers.**

1 Please sit down.

2 Don't open your book.

  3 **Read. Then draw and write.**

_____

My Classroom

There is a board.

There are twenty-nine children.

_____

1 My Day

1 Write the words.

~~have~~   brush   get   go
play   go   have   get   have

1 **have** breakfast

2 _____ to bed

3 _____ lunch

4 _____ dinner

5 _____ to school

6 _____ up

7 _____ dressed

8 _____ your teeth

9 _____ in the park

1 Read, look, and draw the time.

When do you have breakfast?
At eight o'clock.
At eight o'clock.

What time is it?
It's eight o'clock.
It's eight o'clock.

2 What time is it? Read and circle.

1

It's **one** /
(**two**) o'clock.

2

It's **three** /
four o'clock.

3

It's **seven** /
eight o'clock.

4

It's **eleven** /
twelve o'clock.

3 Write and draw the times for you.

1 I get up at __**seven**__ o'clock.

2 I have lunch at _____ o'clock.

3 I have dinner at _____ o'clock.

4 I go to bed at _____ o'clock.

1 🎧 **003** 🛡 **Can you remember? Listen and write**
Brazil, *Turkey*, or *China*.

What time is it in Brazil? …

It's nine o'clock in Brazil.
Nine o'clock is cool.
It's nine o'clock in Brazil.
It's time to go to school.

<u>Turkey</u>

What time is it in Turkey? …

It's three o'clock in Turkey.
My friends are all with me.
It's three o'clock in Turkey.
It's time to watch TV.

_____

What time is it in China? …

It's eight o'clock in China.
The moon is very bright.
It's eight o'clock in China.
It's time to say "goodnight."

_____

_____

2 🛡 **Read and write the times.**

It's seven o'clock in Brazil.

1 What time is it in Turkey?

It's _____ o'clock.

2 What time is it in China?

It's _____ o'clock.

1 **Look and write.**

> goes   goes   has   sleeps   ~~walks~~   watches

Penny **(1)** __walks__ home at seven o'clock.

She **(2)** _____ her dinner at eight.

Then she **(3)** _____ some TV

And **(4)** _____ to bed. It's late!

She's very tired at nine o'clock.

She **(5)** _____ to sleep at ten.

She **(6)** _____ and sleeps, and then It's time to get up again!

2 **Write words to complete the sentences.**

> walks   plays   has   has   goes   ~~gets~~

1 Sam __gets__ up at seven o'clock.

2 Sam _____ breakfast at eight o'clock.

3 Sam _____ to school at nine o'clock.

4 Sam _____ in the park at five o'clock.

5 Sam _____ dinner at six o'clock.

6 Sam _____ to bed at ten o'clock.

1 🎧 004 **Who says it? Listen and check ✓.**

2 🛡 **Look and write the numbers.**

1 Careful, Thunder. **2** Sorry, Mom! **3** Can you see my keys?

3 🛡 **Who says it? Match.**

1 Careful! **2** What's the problem? **3** We can play. Hooray!

Which children are helping? Look and check ☑.

2 005 **Listen and say.**

3 006 **Listen and circle. Point and say.**

 king  qu**ee**n

 p**i**ns  p**ea**s

 chicken  ch**ee**se

 fish  f**ee**t

1 🎧 **007** **Read the questions. Listen and write a name or number.**

1 What's the girl's name? <u>Shelley   </u>.

2 How old is she? <u>   </u>.

3 She gets up at <u>   </u> o'clock.

4 She has breakfast at <u>   </u> o'clock.

5 What's her best friend's name? <u>   </u>.

2 🛡 **Draw and write about someone in your family.**

<u>My dad cooks dinner at</u>
<u>seven o'clock.</u>

1 **Look and read. Write *yes* or *no*.**

1

Paul gets up at six o'clock. __**no**__

2

Paul has two children. _____

3

Paul works at a zoo. _____

4

At one o'clock, Paul has lunch. _____

5

Paul walks home at 5 o'clock. _____

6

Paul has dinner with the children. _____

7

The children go to bed at seven o'clock. _____

8

In the evening, Paul plays soccer. _____

2 **Write two more true sentences about Paul.**

Paul gets up at seven o'clock. _____

_____

1 Look and write.

shadow   sun   ~~sundial~~   Roman numbers

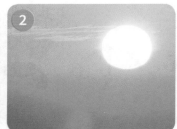
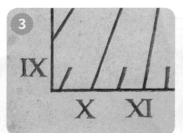

sundial _____   _____   _____

2 Look at the words in Activity 1 and complete the sentences.

(1) This is a __sundial__ . It's old so
(2) it has _____ _____.
(3) The _____ makes a shadow
on the sundial. To know the time, look
(4) at the _____ and read the
Roman numbers.

3 Look and draw lines.

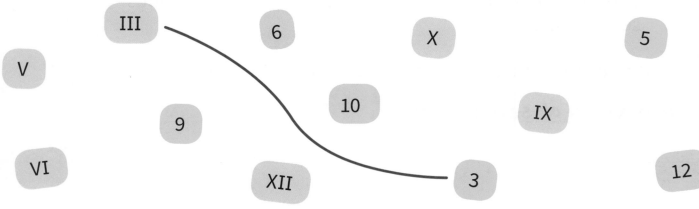

III   6   X   5
V
10   IX
9
VI   XII   3   12

4 Look and write.

Across ➡

a VIII

b IV

c VII

d I

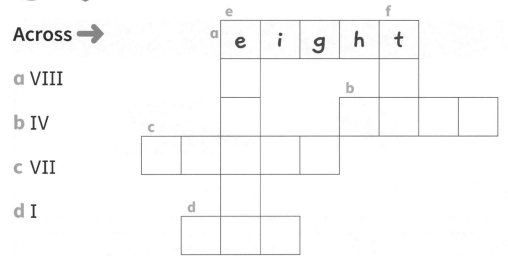

| a e | i | g | h | t |

Down ⬇

e XI

f II

5 Look and write the times.

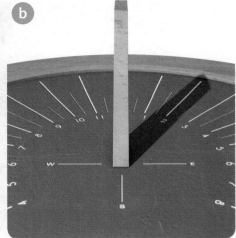

_____ . _____ . _____ .

6 Look at the clocks in Activity 5. Complete the sentences.

(1) I think clock _____ is very old

(2) and clock _____ is old.

(3) I think clock _____ is new.

1 **Make a diary.**

You need

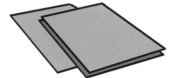

3 sheets of paper   a stapler   pens and pencils

1

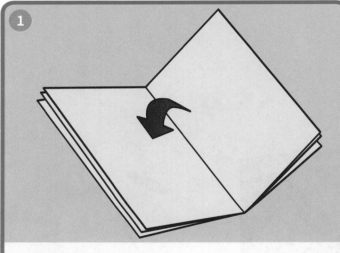

Fold the paper in half.

2

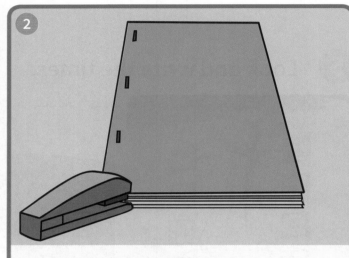

Your teacher staples the paper.

3

Write *My Week* and the days of the week in the diary.

4

Now draw and write in your diary.

What do I know?

1 Write and circle.

1 I can write the names of five daily activities. **Yes / No**

have _____ _____ _____ _____

breakfast _____ _____ _____ _____

2 It's _____ o'clock.

3 Alex _____ at seven o'clock. (get up)

2 Look and write.

BIG QUESTION How do we know the time?

1 s_____

2 s_____

3 R_____
   n_____

4 s_____

 About me!

3 Read. Then draw and write.

I go to school at 9 o'clock. _____

1 Find the animals and write. Look ➡, ⬇, and ↘.

zebra _____ _____

p	c	r	o	c	o	d	i	l	e
a	o	r	s	r	p	b	l	a	t
r	o	z	e	b	r	a	e	d	l
r	m	e	i	n	d	n	a	a	v
o	h	h	m	o	n	k	e	y	r
t	v	i	c	t	d	n	o	h	s
e	i	o	p	d	r	f	h	o	n
s	r	g	s	p	s	s	l	w	a
c	l	s	e	m	o	a	u	x	k
p	o	l	a	r	b	e	a	r	e

_____

_____

_____ _____ _____

1 Read and circle.

(1) Penny **likes** / **doesn't like** fish.

(2) She **likes** / **doesn't like** peas.

Don't give Penny

Any peas, please!

2 Look and write *likes* or *doesn't like*.

Tom _likes_____
bananas.

Ben _____
bananas.

Anna _____
apples.

Grace _____
apples.

Jill _____
milk.

Bill _____
milk.

Can you remember? Listen and write.

| bears | crocodiles | hippos | parrots | ~~snakes~~ | tigers |

(1) ___Snakes___ like grass,
(2) And _____ do, too.
They like life
Here in the zoo.

In the zoo, in the zoo …

(3) _____ like trees,
(4) And _____ do, too.
They like life
Here in the zoo.

In the zoo, in the zoo …

(5) _____ like water,
(6) _____ do, too.
They like life
Here in the zoo.

In the zoo, in the zoo …

2 **Draw and write a new verse.**

_____,

And _____ do, too.

They like life

Here in the zoo.

1 Look, read, and check ☑.

1

a Does Charlie eat bananas for breakfast?

   Yes, he does. ☐   No, he doesn't. ☑

b Does Charlie eat bread for breakfast?

   Yes, he does. ☐   No, he doesn't. ☐

2

a Does Charlie sleep in a bed?

   Yes, he does. ☐   No, he doesn't. ☐

b Does Charlie sleep in a tree?

   Yes, he does. ☐   No, he doesn't. ☐

3

a Does Charlie ride a bike to school?

   Yes, he does. ☐   No, he doesn't. ☐

b Does Charlie walk to school?

   Yes, he does. ☐   No, he doesn't. ☐

2 Look and write *does*, *doesn't*, or *like*.

(1) **Does** Penny (2) _____ crocodiles?

No, she (3) _____ .

(4) _____ Penny (5) _____ polar bears?

(6) Yes, she _____ !

1 🎧 **009** Who says it? Listen and check ✅.

2 Read the story. Then read and check ✅.

1 Does the  catch the  ?
   Yes, he does. ☐
   No, he doesn't. ☐

2 Does catch the  ?
   Yes, she does. ☐
   No, she doesn't. ☐

3 Does  catch the  ?
   Yes, she does. ☐
   No, she doesn't. ☐

3 Look and write the numbers.

1 Come here, Snake.   2 Let's help him!   3 How does he do that?

1 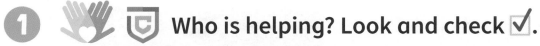 Who is helping? Look and check ☑.

2 What's in Kim's dinner? What's in Mike's pie? Say and write.

> fl**y**   ~~s**i**x~~   sp**i**der   l**i**zard   wh**y**   h**i**ppo   t**i**ger   p**i**n

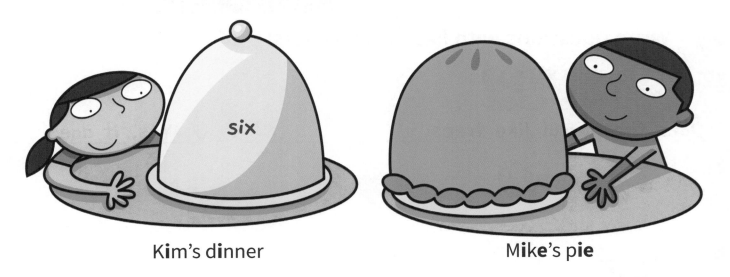

K**i**m's d**i**nner   M**i**ke's p**ie**

3 🎧 010 Listen, say, and check your answers.

1  **Listen and circle.**

1 a Does the bear eat carrots?

~~Yes, it does.~~   No, it doesn't.

b Does the bear come from Canada?

Yes, it does.   No, it doesn't.

2 a Does the hippo come from Africa?

Yes, it does.   No, it doesn't.

b Does the hippo live in the jungle?

Yes, it does.   No, it doesn't.

3 a Does the mouse eat cheese?

Yes, it does.   No, it doesn't.

b And does it live in the jungle?

Yes, it does.   No, it doesn't.

2 **Write questions with *like* and answers.**

1

Does the parrot like trees _____ ? ✓ Yes, it does .

2

_____ ? ✗ _____ .

3

_____ ? ✗ _____ .

4

_____ ? ✓ _____ .

1 Read and complete.

A Zebra

I have four **(1)** <u>legs</u>, two ears, two eyes, and lots of
(2) _____ and white stripes. I come from Africa, but now I live in a
(3) _____. I like carrots and **(4)** _____. I don't like bananas.
I drink **(5)** _____. I have lots of friends here. My best friend is
Charlie. He's a **(6)** _____.

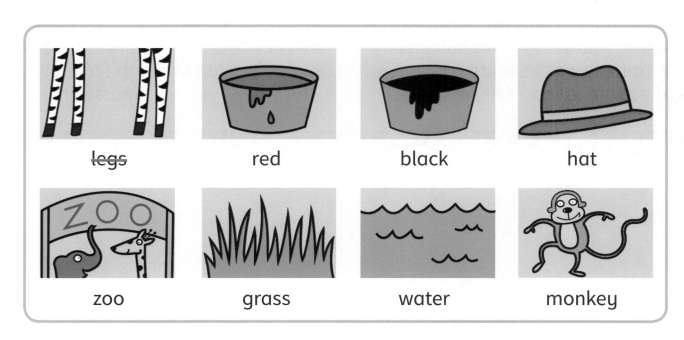

Think and Learn

Habitats

1 **Look and write.**

| grasslands | ~~ocean~~ | polar habitat | rainforest |

1   2   3   4

ocean

2   **Read, look, and write the animals.**

Where do animals live?

Some animals live in one habitat. For example, zebras live in grasslands. Some animals live in two habitats. For example, parrots and tigers can live in the rainforest and the grasslands. And fish can live in the ocean or rainforest. Some animals can live in three habitats! For example, crocodiles and snakes can live in the rainforest, in the ocean, and in the grasslands.

Grasslands	Ocean	Rainforest

3 🛡 Look and write numbers.

1 grasslands   **2** rainforest   **3** ocean   **4** polar habitat

4 Draw two animals in their habitats.

This is a _____.

It lives in _____.

This is a _____.

It lives in _____.

Make a zoo.

You need

paper

yarn

tape and glue

pens and pencils

scissors

1

Draw the head and a rectangle for the body.

2
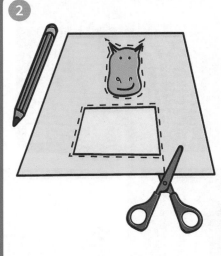
Cut them out.

3

Color and decorate the head and the body.

4
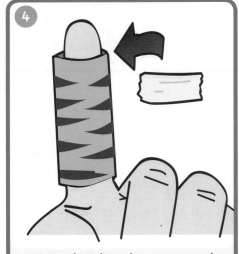
Put the body around your finger with tape.

5

Glue on the head.

6

Now you can make a zoo!

 1 **Write and circle.**

1 I can write the names of five animals.   **Yes / No**

___zebra___   _____   _____   _____   _____

2 The boys **like / likes** milk.

3 The girl **don't like / doesn't like** apples.

2  **Look and write.**

BIG QUESTION **Where do animals live?**

g_____   o_____   r_____   p_____
habitat

 3 **Read. Then draw and write.** _____

My Favorite
Animal

This is a parrot.   _____.

It lives in the rainforest.   _____.

3 Where We Live

1 **Look and draw lines.**

store   hospital   café

movie theater   street

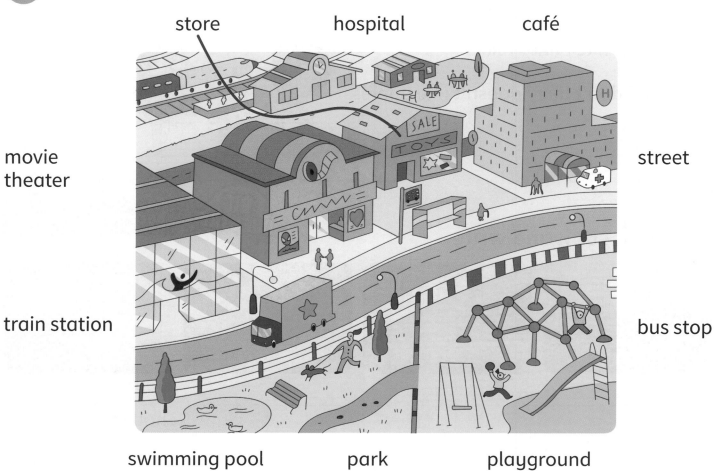

train station   bus stop

swimming pool   park   playground

2 **Match and write the words.**

1 str	ool	**street**	
2 ca	ital		
3 st	rk		
4 pa	fé		
5 hosp	ore		
6 sch	eet		

34 Places in a Town

1 Read and circle.

(1) (Does) / **Do** your town have a movie theater?

(2) No, it **doesn't** / **don't**!

(3) **Does** / **Do** your town have a swimming pool?

(4) Yes, it **does** / **do**!

2 Look, read, and check ✓.

1 Does the town have a swimming pool? Yes, it does. ✓ No, it doesn't. ☐

2 Does the town have a movie theater? Yes, it does. ☐ No, it doesn't. ☐

3 Does the town have a park? Yes, it does. ☐ No, it doesn't. ☐

4 Does the town have a playground? Yes, it does. ☐ No, it doesn't. ☐

5 Does the town have a train station? Yes, it does. ☐ No, it doesn't. ☐

3 Write about your town.

My town has a park and a store. It doesn't have a café.

Can you remember? Listen and write.

✓ = has   ✗ = doesn't have   ? = doesn't say

It's good to have a friend from the town...

Does your town have a playground?
Yes, it does, Sue.
Please tell me how to get there.
I can go there with you.

It's good to have a friend ...

Does your town have a bookstore?
Yes, it does, Jack.
Please tell me how to get there.
I can draw it on my map.

It's good to have a friend ...

Does your town have a café?
No, it doesn't, Jack and Sue.
But let's go to my house.
There's cake and fruit for you.

It's good to have a friend ...

2 Write about the town with *has* and *doesn't have*.

1 The town _____.

2 The town _____.

3 The town _____.

1 Write the words in the correct order.

1 is / The fish / the rock / next to

The fish is next to the rock .

2 in front of / is / the rock / The fish

_____ .

3 behind / is / The fish / the rock

_____ .

4 the tree / is between / and / the fish / The rock

_____ .

2 Read and write the words.

school   toy store   movie theater   bookstore   ~~café~~

1 café _____

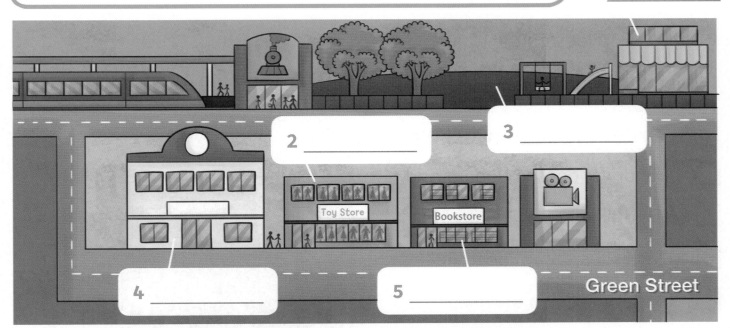

2 _____

3 _____

4 _____

5 _____

Green Street

In our town, the school is on Green Street. It's in front of the train station. There are a lot of stores on Green Street. Next to the school, there's a toy store. There's a bookstore between the toy store and the movie theater.

There's a park behind the stores and the movie theater. In the park, there's a playground and a café. The ice cream there is great!

1 🎧 013 Who says it? Listen and check ✓.

2 Read and match.

1 What's on the track?   a The girl is fast.

2 Who runs to stop the train?   b The driver.

3 What does the driver think?   c A big tree.

4 What idea does Flash have?   d Yes, he does.

5 Does the driver stop the train?   e Flash.

6 Who says "Thanks"?   f She writes, "STOP."

3 Order the sentences. Write numbers.

☐ The driver doesn't understand.

8 The driver says, "Thanks."

4 Flash says, "Stop the train!"

☐ Flash runs down the hill.

☐ The driver stops the train.

☐ They see a tree on the train track.

☐ Flash writes, "STOP."

1 The Super Friends are on a hill.

1 Which boy perseveres? Look and check ☑.

2 Look and write.

| ~~tr~~ | br | tr | gr | cr | dr | dr | br |

1 **t r** ee

2 have ___eakfast

3 get ___ ___essed

4 ___ ___ush your teeth

5 ___ ___ocodile

6 ___ ___andmother

7 ___ ___iver

8 ___ ___ain

3 🎧 014 Listen, say, and check your answers.

1 🎧 **015** **Listen and write S (Sarah), O (Oscar), or C (Cheryl).**

1 Where?

2 With?

3 When?

  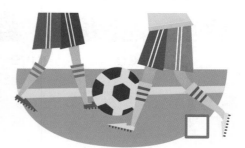

4 What?

2 🛡 **Read and write.**

> I go to my favorite store with my mom on Saturdays. I read a book there every week!

Grace's favorite place is the _____.

1 **Look at the pictures and the letters. Write the words.**

p a r k   r k a p

_ _ _ _ _   t e r s o

_ _ _ _ _ _ _   i o m v e   e t e r a h t

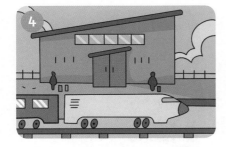

_ _ _ _ _ _   t t n i o a s

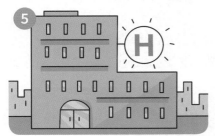

_ _ _ _ _ _ _ _   l p i a h s o t

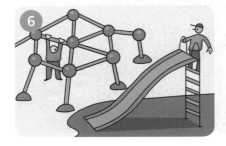

_ _ _ _ _ _ _ _ _   g l d n y a u o r p

Think and Learn

Places in Town

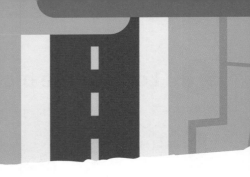

1 Look and write.

> parking lot   ~~market~~   monument   sports center   museum

market _____   _____   _____   _____   _____

2 🛡 **Where can you find each object? Look and draw lines.**

parking lot

market

sports center

museum

3

3 Look and write the letters and numbers.

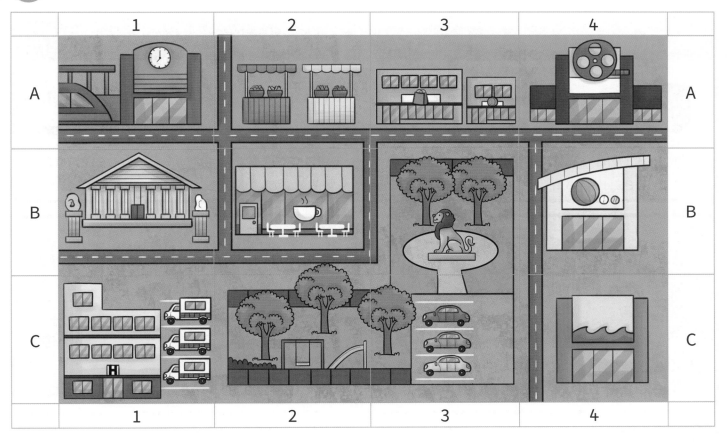

1 swimming pool	**4C**	4 monument	
2 sports center		5 stores	
3 train station		6 parking lot	

4 Look at Activity 3. Write words to complete the puzzle.

1B | m | o | n | u | m | e | n | t |

2B

2C

2C, 3C, 3B

4A

1C

I'm going to the _____!

1 **Make a box town.**

You need

boxes and tubes

tape and glue

colored paper

tissue

scissors

pens and pencils

1

Glue or tape colored paper on the boxes and tubes.

2

Put doors and windows on the box.

3

Add chimneys and use tissue to make smoke.

4

Decorate your building.

5

Now you can make a box town.

1 **Write and circle.**

1 I can write the names of five places in a town.   **Yes / No**

playground _____ _____ _____ _____

2 Does the street have a café?
Yes, it does. / No, it doesn't.

3 The bus stop is **in front of / next to** the movie theater.

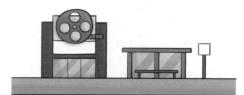

2 **Look, read, and write.**

BIG QUESTION **How can we find places?**

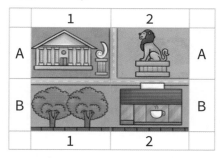

1 What's in 1A?   a _____

2 What's in 2B?   a _____

3 Where's the monument?   It's in _____.

 3 **Read. Then draw and write.** _____

My Favorite Place

I love the café in my town.

I eat ice cream there.

1 Do the crossword.

1

2

3

4

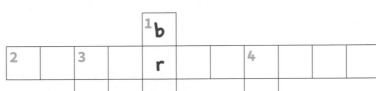

5

The crossword:

1 down: b r e a d

2 across

3 down

4 across

5 down

6 across

7 down

8 down

9 across

10 across

11 across

6

7

8

9

10

11

1 Read and circle.

(1) **Would you** / **Do you** like a pizza, Penny?

Yes, please.

(2) Would you like **a** / **some** bread?

Yes, please.

Would you like some ice cream?

(3) **Yes, please.** / **No, thank you.** I think I need my bed.

2 Write *a*, *an*, or *some*.

1   Would you like __a_____ tomato?   Yes, please.

2   Would you like _____ lemon?   No, thank you.

3   Would you like _____ egg?   Yes, please.

4   Would you like _____ grapes?   No, thank you.

5   Would you like _____ orange?   Yes, please.

3 Write the words in the correct order.

1 you / like / an / Would / orange

    __Would you like an orange__ ?

    Yes, please.

2 a / like / you / mango / Would

    _____ ?

    Yes, please.

3 like / bread / Would / you / some

    _____ ?

    No, thank you.

4 some / like / you / fish / Would

    _____ ?

    No, thank you.

1 🎧 016 🛡 **Can you remember? Listen and write.**

(1) Would you like an 🍎 _____?

(2) Would you like a 🍐 _____?

There's lots of fruit and vegetables,

Lots for us to share.

Super fruit and vegetables,

Pick them from the tree.

(3) Lemons, pears, and 🫒 _____, too.

Pick one for you

And one for me.

Super fruit and vegetables,

Grow them in the ground.

(4) Carrots, 🫛 _____,

(5) 🫘 _____, too.

There's good food all around.

2 🛡 **Draw the food from Activity 1. Where does it grow?**

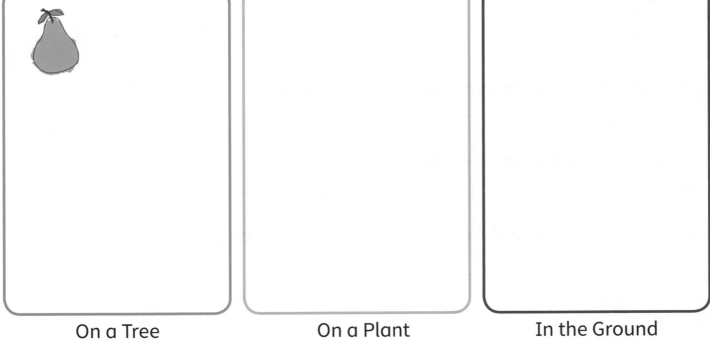

On a Tree   On a Plant   In the Ground

1 Look, read, and check ☑.

1 Are there any grapes?   Yes, there are. ☑   No, there aren't. ☐

2 Are there any lemons?   Yes, there are. ☐   No, there aren't. ☐

3 Are there any watermelons?   Yes, there are. ☐   No, there aren't. ☐

4 Is there any chicken?   Yes, there is. ☐   No, there isn't. ☐

5 Are there any eggs?   Yes, there are. ☐   No, there aren't. ☐

2 Look and circle.

1 **Is** / **Are** there any cheese
in the house?

  a No, there **isn't** / **aren't** any.

  b Yes, there **is** / **are**.

2 **Is** / **Are** there any grapes
in the house?

  a No, there **isn't** / **aren't** any.

  b Yes, there **is** / **are**.

3 Write about your school bag.

There is an apple in my bag. There isn't a mango.

1 🎧 **017** **Who says it? Listen and check ☑.**

2 **Order the sentences. Write numbers.**

☐ Misty has an idea.

☐ The man gives the bag of apples to the children.

`1` Flash gives her friends some apples.

☐ Misty sees two boxes of apples.

☐ The children show everyone the apples!

`5` The children ask for eight apples.

☐ Each friend has one bad apple.

☐ The man puts four good apples and four bad apples in a bag.

3 **Look and write the numbers.**

1 We know what we can do!   **2** What can we do?   **3** Good job!

1  Who is cheating? Look and check ☑.

2 🎧 018 Listen and follow. Say the number.

Start →

1

2

3

4

3 🎧 019 Listen again and say.

1 🎧 **020** **What do they like? Listen and check ☑.**

	Sandra	John	Mom	Dad
(chicken)	✓	✓	✓	✓
(fruit bowl)				
(beans)				
(tomatoes)				
(juice)				
(water)				

2 🛡 **Write about your family.**

Hi, I'm Mei. I live in Beijing. In our family, we often eat pizza. I like orange juice, but my sister doesn't. She likes milk.

1 Look, read, and put a check ☑ or an X ☒.

This is a pear. ☑

This is an orange. ☐

This is a cake. ☐

This is a bean. ☐

This is an egg. ☐

This is a mango. ☐

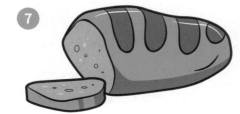

This is some bread. ☐

Think and Learn

WEIGHTS

1 How many grams do they weigh? Look and write.

a four mangoes   _800g_

b five eggs   _____

c four potatoes   _____

d three tomatoes   _____

e ten grapes   _____

f two kiwis   _____

2 Order the weights. Label the chart.

a   75g   b   100g   c   5g   d   200g   e   50g   f   150g

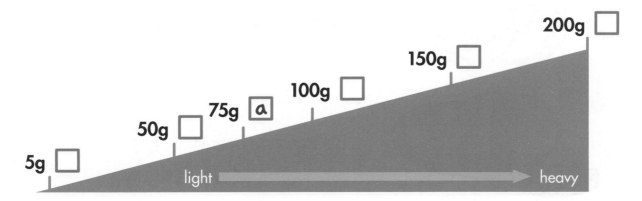

200g ☐

150g ☐

100g ☐

75g [a]

50g ☐

5g ☐

light → heavy

3 **Add the food weights.**

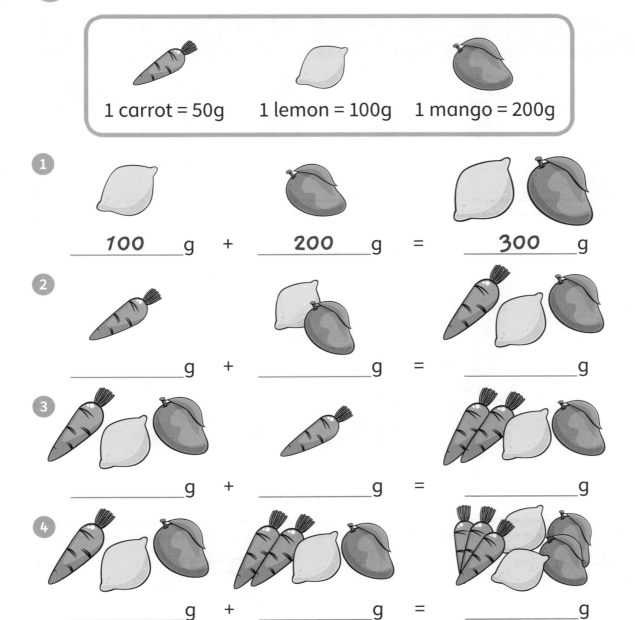

1 carrot = 50g   1 lemon = 100g   1 mango = 200g

1 ___100___ g + ___200___ g = ___300___ g

2 _____ g + _____ g = _____ g

3 _____ g + _____ g = _____ g

4 _____ g + _____ g = _____ g

4 **Look, read, and answer *yes* or *no*.**

500g of watermelon weighs the same as 500g of grapes.

Is it true?

_____

1 **Make a potato person.**

You need

     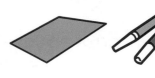

| scissors | clean potatoes | yarn | toothpicks | glue | paper | pens |

1

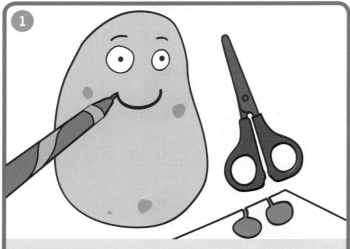

Give your potato a face with pens, glue, and paper.

2

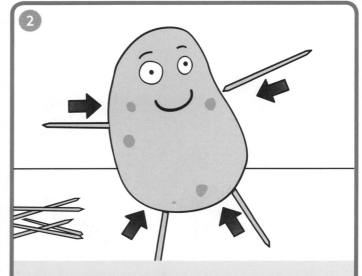

Use toothpicks for arms and legs.

3

Use yarn for hair.

4

Use paper for the clothes.
Now you have a potato person!

1 **What do I know?** **Write and circle.**

1 I can write the names of five foods.   **Yes / No**

__bread__   _____   _____   _____   _____

2 Is there any fruit?

Yes, there is. / No, there isn't.

3 Are there any vegetables?

Yes, there are. / No, there aren't.

2 **Order the sentences. Write numbers.**

 **BIG QUESTION** **How can we buy food?**

a Go to a store, market, or supermarket.   ☐

c Say "thank you" to the salesclerk.   ☐

b Make a shopping list.   ☐ 1

d Say "ten carrots, please" or "500g of carrots."   ☐

3 **About me!** **Read. Then draw and write.** _____

My Favorite Fruit

I love mangoes! I eat them in _____
a fruit salad.   _____

5 My Bedroom

1 **Read and color.**

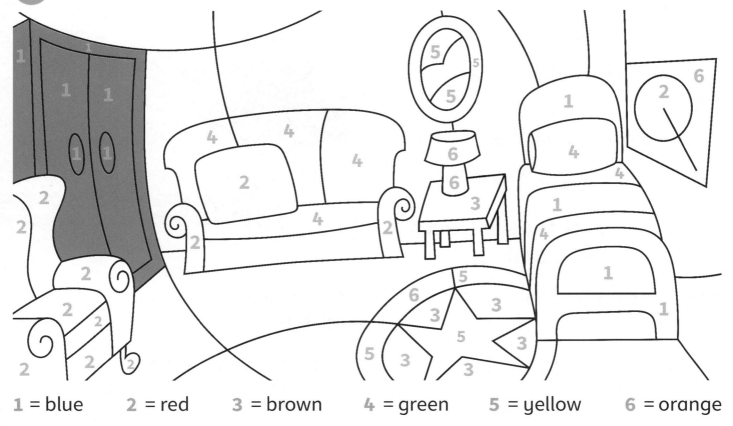

1 = blue   2 = red   3 = brown   4 = green   5 = yellow   6 = orange

2 **Look at Activity 1. Write the words.**

bed   couch   lamp   rug   armchair
mirror   ~~closet~~   table   poster

1 The **closet** is blue.

2 The _____ is orange.

3 The _____ is brown.

4 The _____ is red.

5 The _____ is yellow.

6 The _____ is blue and green.

7 The _____ is red and orange.

8 The _____ is red and green.

9 The _____ is brown, yellow, and orange.

1 Look and draw lines.

a

b

1 I like these armchairs.

2 This bed is fun!

3 I like those rugs.

4 That closet is nice.

c

d

2 Look, read, and circle.

1

2

3

4

These / **Those** chairs are great.

I like **this** / **that** table.

This / **That** mirror is pretty.

I like **these** / **those** armchairs.

3 Write the words in the correct order.

1 this / I / closet / like

   I like this closet_____.

2 chair / like / I / that

   _____.

3 I / posters / these / like

   _____.

4 pretty / those / I / lamps / like

   _____.

1 🎧 **021** 🛡 **Can you remember? Listen and circle.**

(1) Give me a piece of **food** / (**wood**),

Let's see what I can do.

(2) Let's **cut** / **cook** and paint and make

Some furniture for you.

Take that piece of wood,

(3) **Chop** / **Cut** it, and paint it red.

Put it all together now.

(4) Wow! I like this **bread** / **bed**.

Take that piece of wood,

(5) Cut it, and **paint some squares** / **eat some pears**.

Put it all together now.

(6) Wow! I like these **stairs** / **chairs**.

2 🛡 **Draw and write a new verse.**

Take that piece of _____ ,

_____ it, and _____

Put it all together now.

Wow! _____.

1 Look and circle.

(1) Whose shoes are (these)/ this? (3) Whose hat is **these** / **this**?

(2) **It's** / **They're** Penny's shoes. (4) **It's** / **They're** Penny's hat.

2 Follow the lines and write.

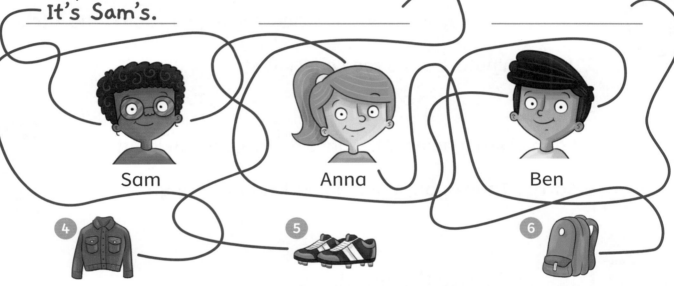

① Whose baseball cap is this?
It's Sam's.

② Whose socks are these?
_____

③ Whose sweater is this?
_____

④ Whose jacket is this?
_____

⑤ Whose soccer cleats are these?
_____

⑥ Whose bag is this?
_____

3 Look and match.

1  Whose boots are these? ☐ It's my pen.

2  Whose pen is this? ☐ No, it's not Jane's. It's mine.

3  Whose bike is this? Is it Jane's? [1] They're Jane's boots.

1 🎧 **022** **Who says it? Listen and check ☑.**

2 **Read and circle.**

1 Sorry, Whisper, not now. She's cleaning up **(her room)** / **the kitchen**.

2 Just a minute. Let me **see** / **check** first.

3 I don't like cleaning. Ah, I have **a problem** / **an idea**!

4 **Sorry** / **Thank you**, Mom. No park for me today.

3 🛡️ **Look and write the numbers.**

1  Finished!

2  Oh, no!

3  Can we eat now?

1  Whose room is clean? Look and check ☑.

2 Say and write the words under *look* or *school*.

~~book~~   pool   zoo   good   food   foot

look

book

_____

_____

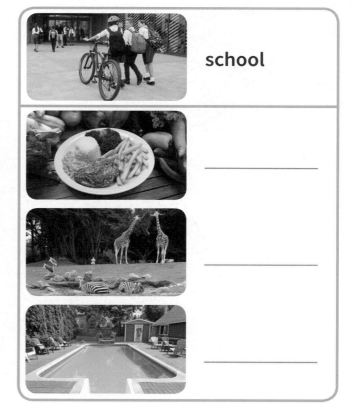

school

_____

_____

_____

3 🎧 023 Listen, say, and check your answers.

🎧 024 **Listen and draw lines.**

Sam   Dan   Alice   Tom

Lucy   Max   Grace

1 Read and write the words.

| are | is | couches |
| sunny | ~~swimming~~ | snow |

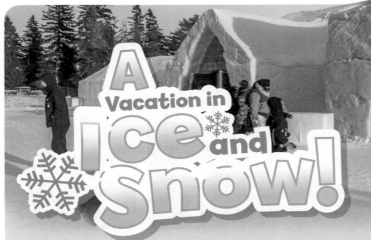

Many people go to hot countries for their vacations. They like
(1) **swimming** in the ocean, and they love the (2) _____ weather.
Other people go to cold countries because they like the (3) _____.
The Ice Hotel is a great place for these people. It is in Canada.

Would you like a vacation at the Ice Hotel? Everything is ice!
There (4) _____ big, beautiful ice lamps. There (5) _____
an ice restaurant, and there are 80 ice
bedrooms. In the bedrooms, there are ice
tables, ice armchairs, ice (6) _____, and,
of course, ice beds too. But don't worry – you
get two very warm sleeping bags for the night!

2 Write about your bedroom.

In my bedroom, there is a big bed, a closet, and there
are two small bookcases. The bed is blue, and the closet
is white. The bookcases are brown.

Materials

1 **Look and write.**

| fabric | glass | metal | plastic | ~~wood~~ |

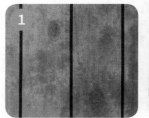    

wood _____ _____ _____ _____

2 **Read and draw lines.**

1 It's made of glass and wood.

2 It's made of metal and plastic. I use it every day!

3 It's made of fabric. It has lots of different colors.

4 It's pretty – it's made of wood and fabric.

5 It's made of wood. I want to paint it!

3 What's in your house? Look, write, and check ☑.

	fabric	glass	metal	plastic	wood
bed	✓				✓

4 Look at Activity 3. Write sentences.

1 My bed is made of fabric and wood_____.

2 _____.

3 _____.

4 _____.

5 Choose, write, and draw.

| fabric   glass   metal   ~~plastic~~   wood |

They're made of _plastic_.

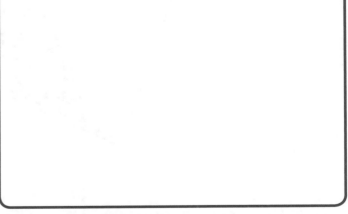

They're made of _____.

1 **Make a picture from paper and plastic.**

You need

a sheet of
card stock

different kinds of
paper and plastic

scissors

glue

Glue the pieces of paper and plastic on the card stock to make your picture.

1 **Write and circle.**

1 I can write the names of five kinds of furniture.   **Yes / No**

armchair   _____   _____   _____   _____

2 Whose baseball cap is **this / these**?
It's / They're Grace's.

3 Whose sneakers are **this / these**?
It's / They're Dan's.

Grace   Dan

 2 **Look, read, and put a check ☑ or an X ☒.**

BIG QUESTION   **What does furniture look like?**

It's made of paper. ☐   It's made of plastic. ☐   It's made of wood. ☐

 3 **Read. Then draw and write.** _____

My Favorite Thing
in My Room

My lamp is red and yellow.   _____
It's made of metal and fabric.   _____

6 People

1 Use the letters to make *face* words.

f~~r~~ e e a h
s n c t~~t~~ s

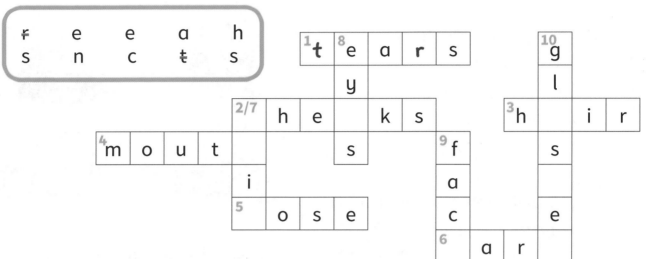

¹t ⁸e a r s ¹⁰g
   y l
²/⁷ h e k s ³h i r
⁴m o u t s s
  i ⁹f
⁵ o s e a e
  c
⁶ a r

2 Write the words.

①

②

③

face _____

④

⑤

⑥

⑦

_____ _____ _____ _____

⑧

⑨

⑩

_____ _____ _____

1 Read and circle.

1

Jill is **sad** / **tired** / (**excited**).

2

Kim is **sad** / **scared** / **happy**.

3

Bill is **tired** / **angry** / **happy**.

4

Sue is **sad** / **happy** / **angry**.

5

Ben is **tired** / **angry** / **sad**.

6

Nick is **angry** / **excited** / **tired**.

2 Look and write.

~~angry~~   excited   happy   tired

(1) Are you __angry__ ?   Are you happy?

No, I'm not angry.   **(3)** Yes, I'm _____

(2) I'm not _____ .   **(4)** and _____ .

1   **025** **Can you remember? Listen and write.**

| ~~face~~ | happy | sad | scared | tired |

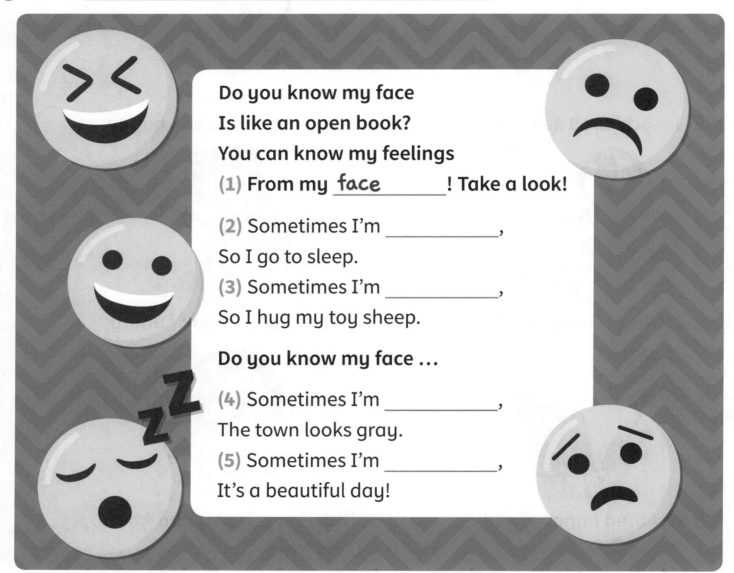

Do you know my face
Is like an open book?
You can know my feelings
(1) From my _face_ ! Take a look!

(2) Sometimes I'm _____,
So I go to sleep.
(3) Sometimes I'm _____,
So I hug my toy sheep.

Do you know my face …

(4) Sometimes I'm _____,
The town looks gray.
(5) Sometimes I'm _____,
It's a beautiful day!

2 **Write a new verse.**

Sometimes I'm _____,
_____.
Sometimes I'm _____,
_____.

happy

excited

sad

scared

angry

tired

1 **Number the months.**

- ☐ April
- ☐ August
- ☐ December
- ☐ February
- 1 January
- 7 July
- ☐ June
- ☐ March
- 5 May
- ☐ November
- ☐ October
- 9 September

2 **Look and match.**

1 My birthday is in April.

2 Their birthdays are in November.

3 Our birthdays are in March.

4 Its birthday is in May.

3 **Look and write.**

(1) O **u r** birthdays aren't in May.

They aren't in September.

(2) O ___ ___ birthdays are in November!

(3) T ___ ___ ___ ___ birthdays aren't in May.

They aren't in September.

(4) T ___ ___ ___ ___ birthdays are in December!

1 🎧 026 **Who says it? Listen and check ☑.**

1

2

3

2 **Look and match.**

1 three-legged race

2 tug of war

3 *Pin the Tail on the Donkey*

a

b

c

3 **Look and write the numbers.**

1 That's not fair!

2 Pull, pull, pull, you can win this tug of war!

3 Oh, no!

a

b

c

1 **Who is being a good loser? Look and check ☑.**

2 **Read and color the train.**

train = **red**   sad = **blue**

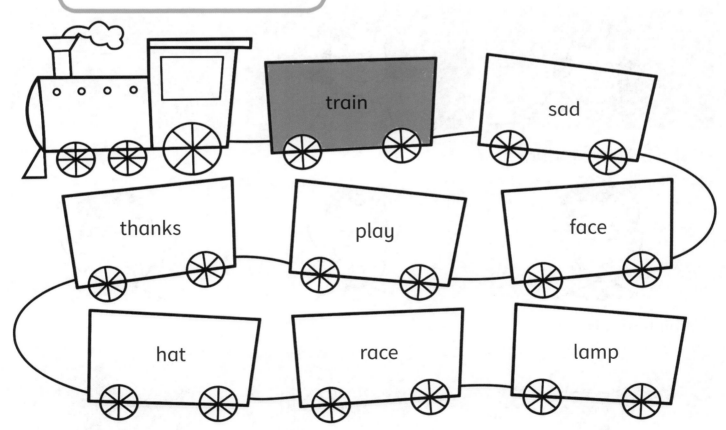

3 **027** **Listen, say, and check your picture.**

Being a Good Loser; Phonics Focus 75

028 **Listen and check** ☑.

1 Who is Emma's best friend?

a ☑   b ☐   c ☐

2 Who is Emma's brother?

a ☐   b ☐   c ☐

3 Who is Jenny?

a ☐   b ☐   c ☐

4 Who is Emma's dad?

a ☐   b ☐   c ☐

5 Which dog is Ben?

a ☐   b ☐   c ☐

1 **Read and write the words.**

38	afternoon	birthday	eleven	soccer
May	park	sister	~~Sunday~~	

1

Dear Sam,

Please come to my birthday party on **(1)** _Sunday_.
It starts at two o'clock. The party is next to the lake
in the **(2)** _____. Can you bring your new
(3) _____ ball? We can play a big game with everyone.

See you there!

Matt

2 PARTY

Dear Finn,

Please come to my
(1) _____ party on
Saturday. It's in the town
hall. You can bring your
(2) _____. She can play
with my little brother. The
party starts at three o'clock in
the **(3)** _____.

See you then!

Emily

3 BIRTHDAY

Dear Lily,

Please come to my birthday
party on Saturday,
(1) _____ 6th. The party
is in our yard, at my house –
(2) _____ Franklin Road.
It starts at **(3)** _____
o'clock in the morning.

Can you come?

Isabel

Portraits

1 **Look and write.**

| drawing | painting | ~~paper collage~~ | photo |

paper collage _____ _____ _____

2 **Read and draw lines.**

1 I'm taking a picture of an angry boy. The angry boy is me!

2 I'm drawing with my friends! We love trees and animals.

3 I'm making a paper collage. It's of my brother and my sister.

4 I have a self-portrait. That's a picture of me! It's a painting.

3 **Look, read, and match.**

1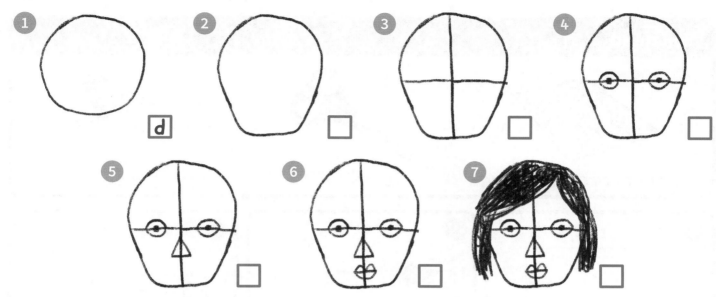
d

2 ☐

3 ☐

4 ☐

5 ☐

6 ☐

7 ☐

a Draw eyes on the line across the middle.

b Add some hair!

c Draw a nose between the eyes and the chin.

d Start with a circle.

e Draw one line down the middle. Then draw one line across the middle.

f Add a chin.

g Draw a mouth in the middle between the nose and the chin.

4 **Look at Activity 3. Draw a self-portrait.**

This is my self-portrait.

I have _____

_____

_____ .

1 Make an emoji birthday card.

You need

a sheet of card stock   scissors   pens

1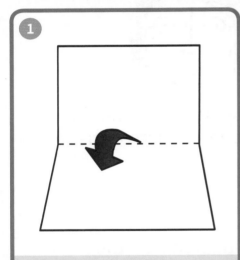

Fold the paper in half.

2

Draw an emoji.

3

Color your emoji.

4

Cut out your emoji. Don't cut on the fold!

5

Happy Birthday Mom

Write on your card.

6

It's an emoji birthday card.

1 **Write and circle.**

1 I can write the names of five parts of the face.   **Yes / No**

_eyes_____   _____   _____   _____   _____

2 Is he sad? **Yes, he is. / No, he isn't.**

3 **His / Their** birthdays are in August.

BIG QUESTION   **How are faces different?**

2 **Look and circle.**

1 Faces can be happy or (sad)/ **drawings**.

2 They can have green eyes or **short / brown** eyes.

3 They can have long or **sad / short** hair.

4 They can be in photos, paper collages, paintings, or **drawings / brown**.

 3 **Read. Then draw and write.**

Today, I feel _**excited**_____

because _**it's my birthday.**_____

Today, I feel _____

because _____

7 Off We Go!

1 🛡 Look at the photos and do the crossword.

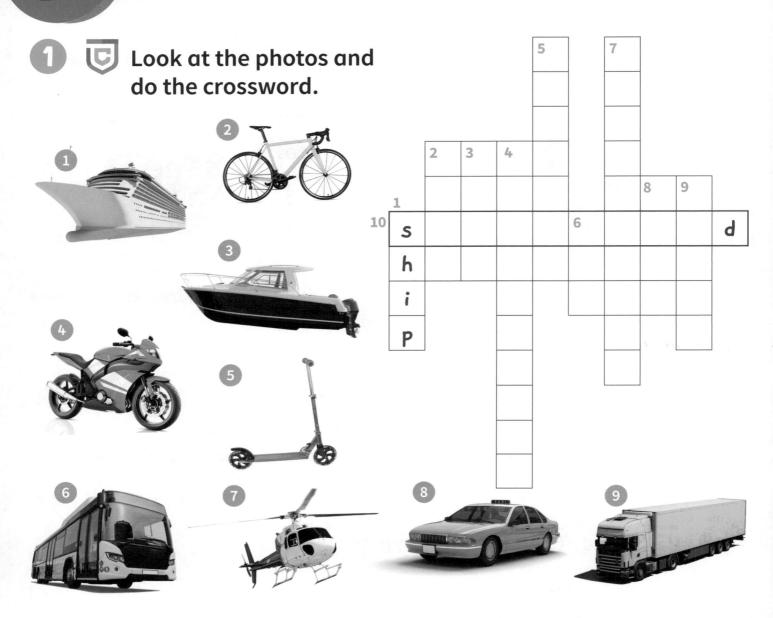

2 Look at Activity 1. Draw number 10.

1 Read and circle.

(1) I'd like **go** / (**to go**) to Brazil by plane!

(2) **I'd** / **I** like to go to Brazil.

(3) I'd like **go** / **to go** to Spain by bus!

(4) **I'd** / **I** like to go to Spain!

2 Read, look, and match.

1 I'd like to fly a helicopter.

2 I'd like to drive a truck.

3 I'd like to sail a boat.

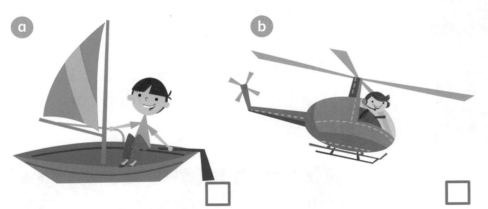

a ☐   b ☐   c ☐

3 Write the words in the correct order.

1 to / I'd / ride / a / motorcycle / like

I'd like to ride a motorcycle .

2 like / sail / a / ship / I'd / to

_____ .

3 I'd / to / a / bus / like / drive

_____ .

4 fly / like / I'd / to / a / plane

_____ .

| car | ~~far~~ | close | plane | skateboard | rocket |

I'd like to go to Africa.

(1) I think it's very **far** _____.

(2) I'd like to go there on a _____.

It's too far for a car.

For a car.

I'd like to go to my friend's house.

It's not so very far.

(3) I'd like to go on my _____.

(4) It's too _____ for a car.

For a car.

I'd like to go to outer space.

I know it's very far.

(5) I'd like to take a _____ there.

(6) It's too far for a _____.

For a car.

2 **Write a new verse.**

I'd like to go to _____.

_____.

I'd like to _____.

It's _____.

1 Complete the questions.

(1) _____ a bus?   (you / drive)

No, I'm not!

(2) What _____?   (you / do)

I'm driving a taxi! Beep! Beep!

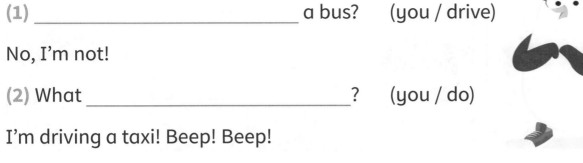

2 Look and draw lines.

1 He's waiting for a bus.

2 She's riding a scooter.

3 He's riding a motorcycle.

4 She's skateboarding.

5 He's sailing a boat.

6 She's riding a bike.

3 Read and match.

1 What are you doing?

2 Are you watching TV?

3 Are you eating chocolate?

4 Is he doing his homework?

5 What is she doing?

6 Is she sleeping?

a ☐ No, I'm not. I'm watching a DVD.

b ☐ Yes, he is.

c ☐ She's taking a shower.

d [1] I'm looking for my bag.

e ☐ No, she isn't.

f ☐ Yes, I am. Would you like some?

1 🎧 030 **Who says it? Listen and check ☑.**

2 **Read and circle. Then read the story and check.**

1 The children are feeling **sad** / **excited**.

2 The children want to go to the **beach** / **airport**.

3 They are on a **plane** / **bus**.

4 First, there are **ships** / **sheep** on the road.

5 Then there is a problem with the **tire** / **window**.

6 Then, they arrive at the **beach** / **airport**.

3 **Look and write the numbers.**

1 Now it's my turn to help you!

2 No problem.

3 I think I can help.

1  Who is being generous? Look and check ☑.

2 Write the letters.

oe   ou   ~~wo~~   ue   oo   ui

t **w** **o**

bl__ __

sh__ __s

y__ __

fr__ __t

sc__ __ter

3 🎧 031 Listen, say, and check your answers.

1 🎧 032 Listen and color.

2 What are they doing? Look at the picture and write.

1 The boy is _____.   2 The girl is _____.

1 **How does Rick travel? Read, look, and draw lines.**

Hi, my name's Rick. I like visiting my friends and family. My cousin Luke lives on a farm with lots of animals. When we visit him, we go by car.

When we visit Grandma Sue, we go by train. She lives in a big city. I love that because I love trains.

When we visit Grandma Pat, we go by plane. She lives in Spain, by the ocean.

My best friend is named Tony. When I go to his house, I ride my bike. He lives on a boat near my house.

1 Luke   2 Sue   3 Pat   4 Tony

a   b   c   d

2 **Read again. Who lives there? Write the names.**

1    2    3    4

Pat

Think and Learn
Transportation

1 Where do they go? Write numbers.

1 in the air

2 on land

3 on water

a

b

c

2 Where are the photos from? Look and write.

in the air   on land   on water

1

2

3

on water

4

5

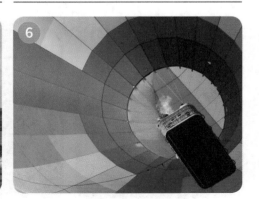
6

3 **What do they need? Write a letter.**

1. I ride a motorcycle. **b**

2. I drive a taxi. ☐

3. I have a canoe. ☐

4. I have a skateboard. ☐

5. I fly a helicopter. ☐

6. I sail a boat. ☐

a

b

c

d

e

f

4 **Choose, draw, and write.**

| in the air | ~~on land~~ | on water |

They go on land.

car

motorcycle

truck

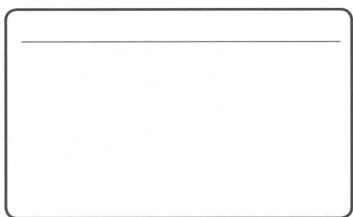

1 Make a speed boat.

You need

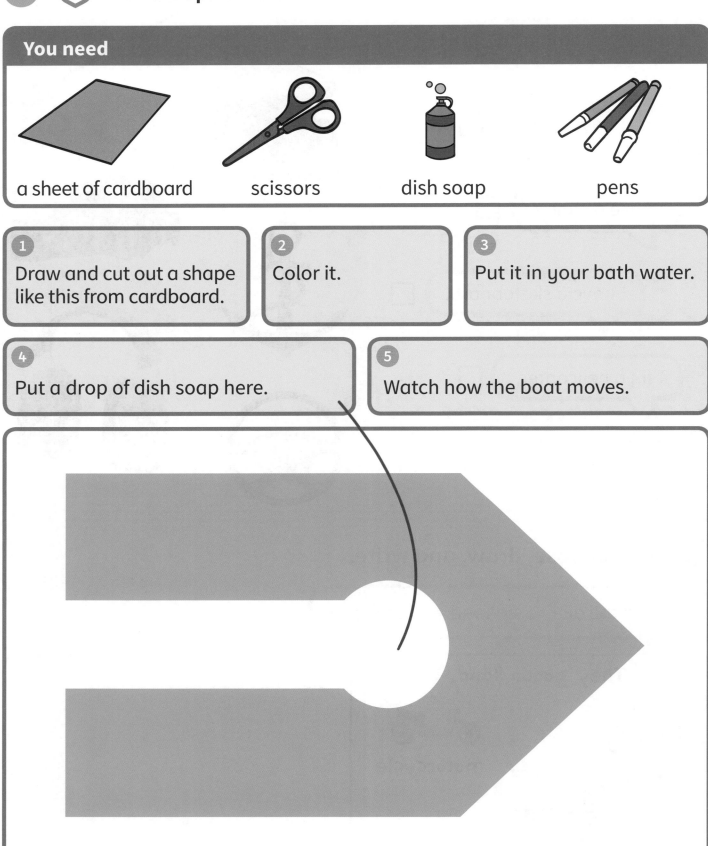

a sheet of cardboard   scissors   dish soap   pens

1 Draw and cut out a shape like this from cardboard.

2 Color it.

3 Put it in your bath water.

4 Put a drop of dish soap here.

5 Watch how the boat moves.

Write and circle.

1 I can write five modes of transportation.   **Yes / No**

helicopter _____ _____ _____ _____

2 I'd like **drive / to drive** a train.

3 Is she riding a bike?
Yes, she is. /
No, she isn't.

---

2 **Look and write.**

BIG QUESTION   **Where can transportation go?**

| in the air   on water   on land |

_____   _____   _____

---

3 **Read. Then draw and write.**

I'd like to sail a ship. _____ _____

8 Sports Center

1 Look and write.

swimming   baseball   soccer   basketball   tennis   volleyball
~~badminton~~   track and field   ping-pong   field hockey

1 <u>badminton</u>

2 _____

3 _____

4 _____

5 _____

6 _____

7 _____

8 _____

9 _____

10 _____

1 Write -ing forms of the words.

| ~~fly~~ | listen | make | paint | play | read | ride | watch |

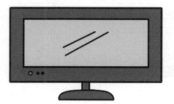

1 __flying__ a kite   2 _____ pictures   3 _____ TV

4 _____ a sandcastle   5 _____ to music   6 _____ horses

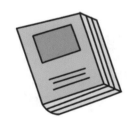

7 _____ a book   8 _____ a guitar

2 Read and write.

(1) Playing soccer's __fun_____ .   (n u f)

Dancing's great.

(2) Flying a kite's _____ .   (d t u f i c l i f)

(3) But swimming's _____ !   (y e s a)

3 Write sentences for you.

1 _____ is great!   2 _____ is boring.

1 🎧 033 🛡 **Can you remember? Listen and match.**

(1) __Playing__ sports is easy.

It's all I want to do.

I'd like to play with you.

(2) Playing sports is great _____.

It's all I want to do.

I'd like to play with you.

Give me a field,

Give me some friends,

(3) Give me a _____ to play.

Now we need two goals.

Let's play soccer all day.

Give me a court,

(4) Give me some _____,

Give me a ball to play.

Now we need a net.

(5) Let's _____ volleyball all day.

2 **Look at Activity 1. Write the words.**

ball   fun   friends   play   ~~playing~~

1 Read and circle.

(1) What sport do you like **play** / (**playing**)?

(2) I like **play** / **playing** soccer.

So do I.

(3) I like **play** / **playing** tennis.

Me, too!

(4) I like **swim** / **swimming**.

I don't. No, no, no!

2 Write the words.

What sport do you like playing?

(2) Me, too! Do you like _____ _____?

(3) I don't. I like _____ _____.

Yes, I do.

(5) Do you like _____ _____?

(1) I like **playing field hockey** _____.

Yes, I do.

(4) So do I. Do you like _____ _____?

(6) No, I don't. I like _____ _____.

1 🎧 **034** **Who says it? Listen and check ☑.**

2 **Read and check ☑ the boxes.**

1 Flash wants to play soccer.   yes ☑   no ☐

2 At first, the boy wants Flash on his team.   yes ☐   no ☐

3 Misty wants to join the ping-pong club.   yes ☐   no ☐

4 Misty scores a goal.   yes ☐   no ☐

5 The green team wins the soccer game.   yes ☐   no ☐

6 At the end, the boy wants Flash on his team.   yes ☐   no ☐

3 **Look and write the numbers.**

1 Ha, ha. It's going to be very easy.

2 Good job, Flash!

3 Join our team!

1  **Who is including people? Look and check ☑.**

2 **Read and color the sock.**

field hockey = **orange**   hippo = **yellow**

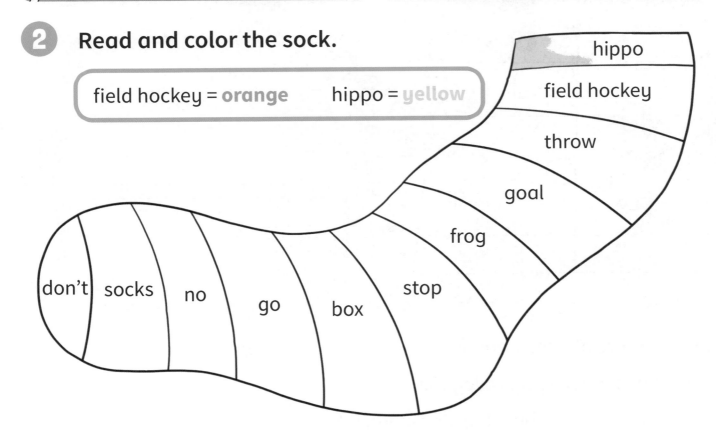

3 🎧 **035** **Listen, say, and check your picture.**

1 Look and read. Write *yes* or *no*.

1 Two boys are playing badminton.   yes

2 Some boys are playing volleyball.   _____

3 There's a woman behind the ping-pong table.   _____

4 A woman is taking a photo.   _____

5 The man has a dog.   _____

6 The tennis players are wearing baseball caps.   _____

1 🎧 036 **Listen and complete. Write one word in each space.**

1 What club does the boy want to join?
  <u>Badminton</u>.

2 When does the club meet?
  Mondays and _____.

3 Where does the club meet?
  In the school _____.

4 Who is the club for?
  _____.

2 **Look and write sentences.**

1 <u>One boy is playing baseball.</u>   3 _____

2 _____   4 _____

Think and Learn

Sports Equipment

1 **Look and write.**

bat board goggles ~~helmet~~ net racket

1 helmet 2 _____ 3 _____ 4 _____ 5 _____ 6 _____

2 **Read, think, and write.**

tennis baseball badminton ~~soccer~~ volleyball

	racket	bat	net	ball
1 soccer				✓
2 _____	✓		✓	
3 _____		✓		✓
4 _____	✓		✓	✓
5 _____			✓	✓

3 **Look and write** *court*, *field*, **or** *track*.

1. track
2. _____
3. _____
4. _____
5. _____
6. _____

4 **Read and draw lines.**

1. tennis   2. skiing   3. surfing   4. swimming

a. I have my goggles, and I'm going to the pool.

b. I have my board, and I'm going to the beach.

c. I have my racket and ball, and I'm going to the court.

d. I have my goggles and my helmet, and I'm going to the mountains.

5 **Choose, draw, and write.**

bat   field   goggles   helmet   net   ~~ball~~

You need a ball for ...

baseball   soccer

1 Make a *Ball in the Cup* game.

You need

pencil   paper cup   string   foil   scissors

1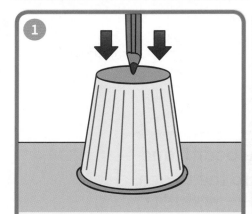

Make a hole in the bottom of the cup.

2

Put some string through the hole.

3

Tie a knot.

4

Make a foil ball at the end of the string.

5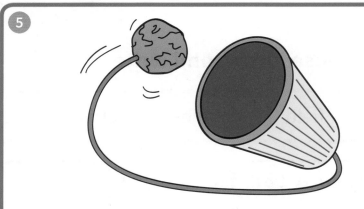

Now play the *Ball in the Cup* game!

1 **Write and circle.**

1 I can write five sports.   **Yes** / **No**

__badminton__   _____   _____   _____   _____

2 I like **ride** / **riding** my bike.

3 What do you like **do** / **doing**?

I like **play** / **playing** the guitar.

BIG QUESTION   **What do we need to play sports?**

 2 **Look and write.**

| track | helmet | net | ~~ball~~ | court | ~~field~~ |

1

2

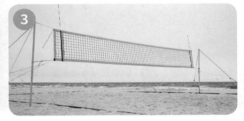
3

__ball__   __field__   _____   _____   _____

---

 3 **Read. Then draw and write.**

I like listening to music.

Singing is fun.

_____

_____

9 Vacation Plans

1 Use the code to write the words.

Things to Do This Summer

1 _l_ _e_ _a_ _r_ _n_ to swim

2 visit my __ __ __ __ __ __ __

3 take __ __ __ __ __ __ __ __ __ __ __ __ __

4 __ __ __ __ __ a tree __ __ __ __ __

5 go __ __ __ __ __ __ __

6 go __ __ __ __ __ __

7 __ __ __ __ a __ __ __ __

8 __ __ __ __ in the __ __ __ __

9 __ __ __ __ a __ __ __ __ __ __ __ __ __ __

Code
a = (briefcase)
b = (bird)
c = (butterfly)
d = (flower)
e = (guitar)
f = (palm tree)
g = (umbrella)
h = (tent)
i = (lizard)
k = (sailboat)
l = (cap)
m = (flip-flops)
n = (camera)
o = (pizza)
p = (ice cream)
r = (dolphin)
s = (leaf)
t = (sun)
u = (popsicle)
y = (life ring)

1 Read and write.

go   build   take

(1) Can I _____ a tree house?

Yes, of course you can.

(2) Can I _____ horseback riding lessons?

Yes, of course you can.

(3) Can we _____ fishing?

Yes, of course we can.

2 Look and write.

1 Can we g_____ h_____ ? 2 Can I g_____ c_____ ?

3 Write the words in the correct order.

1 we / cousins / our / Can / visit

   Can we visit our cousins _____ ?

2 I / Can / to / learn / swim

   _____ ?

3 scrapbook / a / I / Can / keep

   _____ ?

4 help / yard / we / the / Can / in

   _____ ?

1 🎧 037 🛡 Can you remember? Listen and circle.

(1) We all need a (vacation) / amusement **park.**

A time for play and rest.

(2) Sun and **tea / ocean** – come with me.

Vacations are the best.

(3) Can we build a **tree house / sandcastle**?

Can we skip and run?

(4) Can we visit **grandparents / cousins**?

We want to have some fun.

(5) Can we **read a comic book / ride a bike**?

Can we bake a cake?

(6) Can we **eat ice cream / keep a scrapbook**?

We want to take a break.

2 🛡 Write a new verse.

Can we _____?   Can we _____?

Can we _____?   We want to _____.

1 Read and circle.

1 Does your brother like tennis?

a Yes, he does.　　　　b Yes, he is.　　　　c No, he does.

2 How old is Lucy?

a It's eight.　　　　b November.　　　　c She's seven.

3 Do you have a skateboard?

a Yes, I am.　　　　b No, I don't.　　　　c Yes, I can.

4 When do you get up?

a At seven o'clock.　　　　b Yes, I do.　　　　c On the couch.

5 Whose sock is this?

a It's purple.　　　　b It's mine.　　　　c They're mine.

6 Where is the playground?

a Between the school and the stores.　　　　b Yes, it's great.　　　　c Behind the closet.

7 Would you like a kiwi?

a Yes, I do.　　　　b Yes, I can.　　　　c No, thank you.

8 Are there any mangoes in the fridge?

a Yes, there is.　　　　b No, there are.　　　　c Yes, there are.

2 Color in the box for each answer in Activity 1. Find the hidden message.

	1	2	3	4	5	6	7	8
a	g	e	n	d	c	o	n	a
b	z	a	o	k	w	i	t	o
c	s	o	m	j	b	u	r	k

The hidden message is: g_____ _____!

1 🎧 038 **Who says it? Listen and check ☑.**

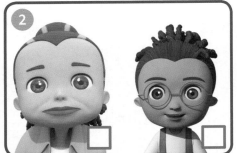

2 **What would they like to do? Read the story and draw lines.**

1 Flash would like to   build a treehouse.

2 Misty would like to   help her grandma in the yard.

3 Thunder would like to   visit her cousins.

3 **Look and write the numbers.**

1 Here you go, Grandma.

2 Can we come up?

3 And what would you like to do, Whisper?

1   **Who is working as a team? Look and check ☑.**

2 🎧 039 **Listen and write the words under *z* or *s*.**

> ~~nose~~   hou**s**e   **z**ebra   **s**wim   le**ss**on
> li**z**ard   tenni**s**   tomatoe**s**

z	s
nose _____ _____	_____ _____
_____	_____

3 🎧 040 **Listen, say, and check your answers.**

1 **Look and read. Write the answers.**

1 Where are the boy and the girl? in a **tree** _____

2 What is the boy wearing on his head? a _____

3 What are they building? a _____

4 Where are they now?   in the _____

5 What does the girl have in her hand?   a _____

6 Where are they now?   in the _____

7 How many sandwiches are there?   _____

Think and Learn

Helping the Environment

1 **Look and write.**

| natural environment | path | recycle | ~~recycling bins~~ | trash |

recycling
bins

_____ _____ _____ _____

2 **How can we help the environment on vacation?**
Read and check ☑.

Do ...	Don't ...	
☑	☐	recycle your trash.
☐	☐	walk on the plants and flowers.
☐	☐	take your trash home.
☐	☐	play with the animals.
☐	☐	leave your trash on the ground.
☐	☐	walk on the path.
☐	☐	learn about the animals in their environment.

3 **What activities can we do? Look and write.**

| build a sandcastle | go fishing | go hiking | go swimming |
| go climbing | look for shells | take horseback riding lessons | take a photo |

Beach	Mountains	Lake
build a sandcastle		

4 **Choose, draw, and write.**

| mountains | beach | ~~lake~~ |

At a lake, you can ...

go fishing

take a photo

go swimming

1 Make a vacation mobile.

You need

 paper   scissors    pens   string   2 clean twigs   pencil

1

Draw four pictures of your favorite vacation activities.

2

Color and cut them out.

3

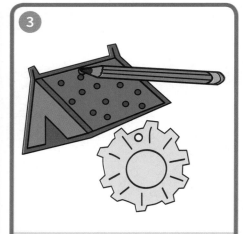

Use a pencil to make a hole on top of each drawing.

4

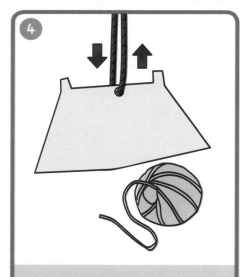

Tie some string to each picture.

5

Tie the two twigs together.

6

Tie your pictures to the twigs to make your mobile.

1 Write and circle.

1 I can write five vacation activities.   **Yes / No**

go hiking   _____   _____   _____   _____

_____   _____   _____   _____

2 _____ we build a tree house?

Yes, of course you **can / can't**.

3 _____ I take horseback riding lessons?

No, sorry. You **can / can't**.

2 Read and circle.

BIG QUESTION What makes a good vacation?

Have a good vacation and help the **(1) natural environment / trash,** too.

Put your **(2) path / trash** in the **(3) recycling bin / trash**.

Walk on the **(4) natural environment / path,** not on the plants and flowers!

About me!

3 Read. Then draw and write.

My favorite vacation activity _____

is camping. _____

Back to School

floor   wall   crayon   bookcase   clock
window   cabinet   ~~board~~   chair   clock   door

board

_____

_____

_____

_____

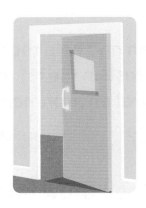

_____

_____

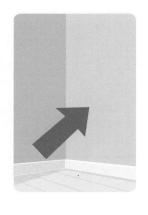

_____

_____

_____

Back to School (continued)

sixty   ~~ten~~   thirty   ninety   forty   one hundred
seventy   eighty   fifty   twenty

10

ten _____

20

_____

30

_____

40

_____

50

_____

60

_____

70

_____

80

_____

90

_____

100

_____

1 My Day

get up   have dinner   get dressed   go to bed   go to school
have lunch   ~~brush your teeth~~   have breakfast   play in the park

brush your teeth

_____

_____

_____

_____

_____

_____

_____

_____

2 The Zoo

polar bear   zebra   ~~bear~~   crocodile   snake
hippo   parrot   tiger   monkey

bear

3 Where We Live

swimming pool   park   hospital   café   playground
store   train station   street   movie theater   ~~bus stop~~   school

bus stop

_____

_____

_____

_____

_____

_____

_____

_____

_____

_____

 **The Market**

watermelons   potatoes   bread   eggs   greens

lemons   ~~beans~~   mangoes   kiwis   tomatoes   grapes

beans

5 My Bedroom

couch   poster   mirror   bed   rug
closet   ~~armchair~~   table   lamp

armchair

_____

_____

_____

_____

_____

_____

_____

_____

6 People

nose   glasses   eyes   face   ~~cheeks~~
hair   chin   tears   mouth   ears

cheeks

_____

_____

_____

_____

_____

_____

_____

_____

_____

ship   taxi   bus   motorcycle   ~~boat~~
scooter   skateboard   helicopter   truck

boat _____

_____

_____

_____

_____

_____

_____

_____

_____

8 Sports Center

basketball   ~~track and field~~   soccer   swimming   field hockey
badminton   ping-pong   volleyball   tennis   baseball

track and field

_____

_____

_____

_____

_____

_____

_____

_____

_____

9 Vacation Plans

visit cousins   help in the yard   go hiking   learn to swim
read a comic book   keep a scrapbook   take horseback
riding lessons   ~~build a tree house~~   go camping

build a
tree house

_____
_____

_____
_____

_____
_____

_____
_____

_____
_____

_____
_____

_____
_____

_____
_____